# The UNITED STATES PRESIDENTS

# Franklin
# PIERCE

BreAnn Rumsch

**Big Buddy Books**
An Imprint of Abdo Publishing
abdopublishing.com

# abdopublishing.com

Published by Abdo Publishing, a division of ABDO, PO Box 398166, Minneapolis, Minnesota 55439.
Copyright © 2017 by Abdo Consulting Group, Inc. International copyrights reserved in all countries. No part of this book may be reproduced in any form without written permission from the publisher. Big Buddy Books™ is a trademark and logo of Abdo Publishing.

Printed in the United States of America, North Mankato, Minnesota
062016
092016

THIS BOOK CONTAINS
RECYCLED MATERIALS

Design: Sarah DeYoung, Mighty Media, Inc.
Production: Mighty Media, Inc.
Editor: Lauren Kukla
Cover Photograph: Getty Images
Interior Photographs: Alamy (p. 9); AP Images (p. 13); Corbis (pp. 5, 7, 15, 21, 23); Getty Images (pp. 6, 11, 25); Library of Congress (p. 19); National Archives (p. 27); North Wind (pp. 7, 17); Public Domain (p. 29)

**Cataloging-in-Publication Data**

Names: Rumsch, BreAnn, author.
Title: Franklin Pierce / by BreAnn Rumsch.
Description: Minneapolis, MN : Abdo Publishing, [2017] | Series: United States presidents | Includes bibliographical references and index.
Identifiers: LCCN 2015044097 | ISBN 9781680781120 (lib. bdg.) | ISBN 9781680775327 (ebook)
Subjects: LCSH: Pierce, Franklin, 1804-1869--Juvenile literature. 2. Presidents--United States--Biography--Juvenile literature. | United States--Politics and Government--1853-1857--Juvenile literature.
Classification: DDC 973.6/6092092 [B]--dc23
LC record available at http://lccn.loc.gov/2015044097

# Contents

# Franklin Pierce

Franklin Pierce became the fourteenth US president in 1853. During his term, he helped **expand** America. He also opened trade between the United States and Japan.

While Pierce was president, slavery **divided** the nation. Pierce did not agree with slavery. However, he believed it was **legal** according to the US **Constitution**.

President Pierce tried his best to be a strong leader. He led the nation through a **challenging** time in history.

# Timeline

### 1804

On November 23, Franklin Pierce was born near Hillsborough, New Hampshire.

### 1837

Pierce was elected to the US Senate.

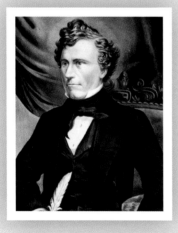

### 1833

Pierce was elected to the US House of **Representatives**.

### 1846

The **Mexican-American War** began in April. Pierce joined the US Army.

**1853**
On March 4, Pierce became the fourteenth US president.

**1848**
The **Mexican-American War** ended with the signing of the **Treaty** of Guadalupe Hidalgo.

**1869**
Franklin Pierce died on October 8.

7

# New Hampshire Boy

Franklin Pierce was born on November 23, 1804, near Hillsborough, New Hampshire.

His parents were Benjamin and Anna Pierce.

Franklin first went to a local school. Then, when he was 11, he began going to schools around New Hampshire.

## ★ FAST FACTS ★

**Born:** November 23, 1804

**Wife:** Jane Means Appleton (1806–1863)

**Children:** three

**Political Party:** Democrat

**Age at Inauguration:** 48

**Years Served:** 1853–1857

**Vice President:** William R.D. King

**Died:** October 8, 1869, age 64

Franklin's childhood home was built by his father, Benjamin Pierce. Benjamin taught Franklin to respect his country and US law.

PIERCE HOMEST

The Pierce Homestead was 1804 by Benjamin Pierce, in the American Revolutio governor of New Hampshire 1829-30), and father of Pierce, the 14th Preside United States (1853-57). Pierce was born in Hillsbo ber 23, 1804 and the famil this dwelling shortly

# Future Leader

In 1820, Pierce entered Bowdoin College in Brunswick, Maine. He **graduated** four years later. He was at the top of his class.

After college, Pierce studied law for three years. In 1827, he opened a law firm in Concord, New Hampshire. Pierce worked hard. He became a successful **lawyer**.

Soon Pierce decided to enter **politics**. In 1829, he was elected to the New Hampshire state **legislature**. Then in 1831, he became **speaker** of the state legislature's lower house.

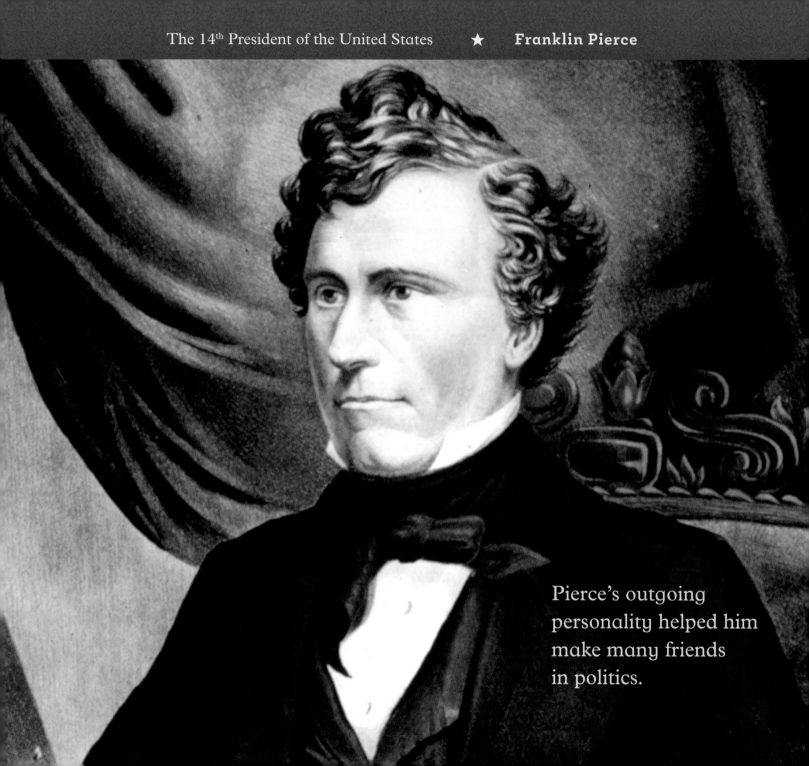

Pierce's outgoing personality helped him make many friends in politics.

# Family and Politics

Pierce continued to find success in **politics**. In 1833, he was elected to the US House of **Representatives**.

While Pierce was serving in the House, the country was split over slavery. Pierce believed the **abolition** movement threatened peace in the United States.

Meanwhile, Pierce married Jane Means Appleton in 1834. The Pierces had three sons. Sadly, all three died before Pierce became president.

Mrs. Pierce with the couple's son Benjamin. Like Pierce, she was from New Hampshire.

# Senator Pierce

In 1837, Pierce was elected to the US Senate. However, Mrs. Pierce eventually grew unhappy with life in Washington, DC. So, in 1842, Pierce left the Senate. He moved his family back to Concord.

In 1844, Pierce helped **Democrat** James K. Polk run for president. Pierce ran the campaign in New Hampshire. Polk won the election. As president, Polk **rewarded** Pierce. He made Pierce New Hampshire's **district attorney**.

Pierce's Concord home is called the Pierce Manse. It opened to the public in 1974.

# Off to War

Meanwhile, Texas had claimed independence from Mexico. In 1845, the United States made Texas a state. This angered Mexico. In addition, Mexico and the United States could not agree on Texas's southern border.

In April 1846, the **Mexican-American War** began. Pierce joined the US Army. He helped **recruit** other men to join the army, too. Soon, he was promoted to colonel and then brigadier general.

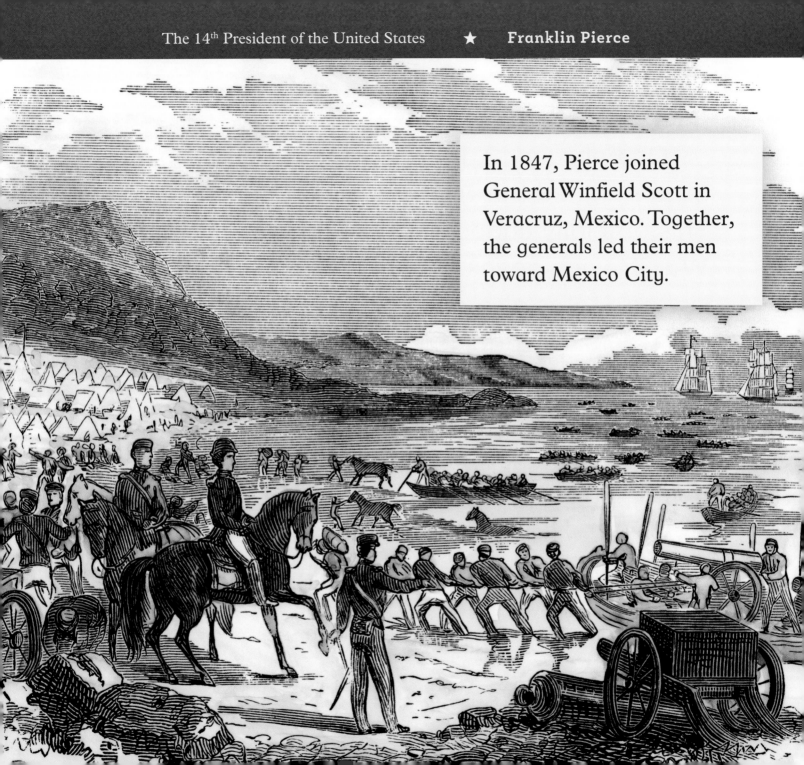

In 1847, Pierce joined General Winfield Scott in Veracruz, Mexico. Together, the generals led their men toward Mexico City.

On February 2, 1848, Mexico and the United States signed the **Treaty** of Guadalupe Hidalgo. This officially ended the **Mexican-American War**. Mexico gave up its claim to Texas. The United States also gained land now making up California, Nevada, and Utah. It also includes parts of Arizona, New Mexico, Colorado, and Wyoming.

After the war, Pierce left the army. He went home to Concord. There, he became a leader in the **Democratic** Party.

★ DID YOU KNOW? ★

Pierce is an ancestor of Barbara Bush, the wife of former president George H.W. Bush.

In 1847, Pierce was thrown from his horse during the Battle of Churubusco. He injured his knee. Yet, he remained with his troops while he recovered.

# The 1852 Election

In June 1852, the **Democrats** chose Pierce to run for president. At this time, slavery continued to **divide** the nation. Pierce did not personally agree with slavery. But, he felt each state should have the right to decide if slavery were **legal**.

Many other Democrats believed Pierce's view would draw more voters. So, Pierce ran against **Whig Party** candidate Winfield Scott. Pierce won the election!

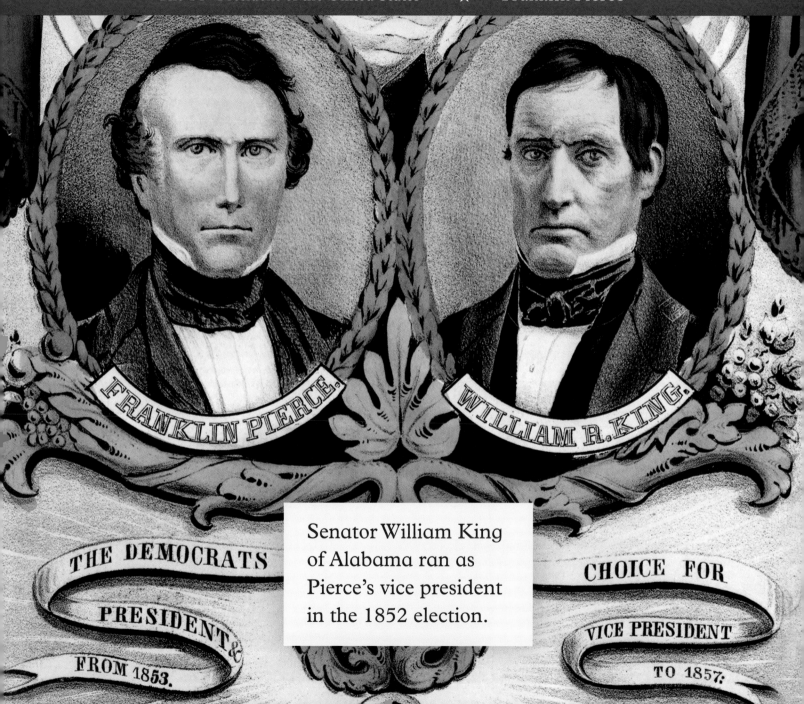

FRANKLIN PIERCE. WILLIAM R. KING.

THE DEMOCRATS

PRESIDENT &

FROM 1853.

CHOICE FOR

VICE PRESIDENT

TO 1857.

Senator William King of Alabama ran as Pierce's vice president in the 1852 election.

# President Pierce

On March 4, 1863, Pierce became president. Shortly after taking office, President Pierce helped **expand** the nation. He ordered the purchase of land west of Texas from Mexico.

The United States got nearly 30,000 square miles (78,000 sq km) of land. Today, this land makes up southern New Mexico and Arizona.

The United States paid Mexico $10 million for the land.

**★ SUPREME COURT ★**
**APPOINTMENTS**

John Archibald Campbell: 1853

On the day he became president, Pierce traveled by carriage in a parade.

# Foreign Affairs

Pierce continued to have success with **foreign** countries. He signed a **treaty** allowing the United States to fish off Canadian coasts. Then, in 1854, the United States and Japan signed a treaty. It allowed the two countries to trade for the first time.

That same year, Pierce hoped to acquire Cuba from Spain. But many Americans were against this. They worried Cuba would become a slave state. Pierce did not want to **divide** the nation further. So, in 1855, he gave up his plan.

# PRESIDENT PIERCE'S CABINET

## March 4, 1853–March 4, 1857

- ★ **STATE:** William Learned Marc
- ★ **TREASURY:** James Guthrie
- ★ **WAR:** Jefferson Davis
- ★ **NAVY:** James Cochran Dobbin
- ★ **ATTORNEY GENERAL:** Caleb Cushing
- ★ **INTERIOR:** Robert McClelland

# Trouble in Kansas

In 1854, Pierce **supported** the Kansas-Nebraska Act. Congress hoped it would settle the slavery question. The act made Kansas and Nebraska new territories. It also said the territories could decide whether or not to have slavery.

However, Kansas soon had two governments. One was pro-slavery. The other was anti-slavery. Settlers fought over which government was right. Pierce sent troops in to help the pro-slavery government.

The Kansas-Nebraska Act became law on May 30, 1854.

# Final Years

The fighting in Kansas slowed. But it did not stop. Many people no longer believed Pierce was a strong enough leader. So, he was not chosen to run for president in 1856.

In 1860, the Pierces moved back to New Hampshire. Pierce returned to his law practice. Then, on October 8, 1869, Franklin Pierce died.

While president, Pierce showed strong leadership. But, he also faced many **challenges**. Still, Franklin Pierce tried his best to keep the country he loved together.

Franklin Pierce
is buried in
the Old North
Cemetery in
Concord.

# Office of the President

## Branches of Government

The US government has three branches. They are the executive, legislative, and judicial branches. Each branch has some power over the others. This is called a system of checks and balances.

### ★ Executive Branch

The executive branch enforces laws. It is made up of the president, the vice president, and the president's cabinet. The president represents the United States around the world. He or she also signs bills into law and leads the military.

### ★ Legislative Branch

The legislative branch makes laws, maintains the military, and regulates trade. It also has the power to declare war. This branch includes the Senate and the House of Representatives. Together, these two houses form Congress.

### ★ Judicial Branch

The judicial branch interprets laws. It is made up of district courts, courts of appeals, and the Supreme Court. District courts try cases. Sometimes people disagree with a trial's outcome. Then he or she may appeal. If a court of appeals supports the ruling, a person may appeal to the Supreme Court.

## Qualifications for Office

To be president, a candidate must be at least 35 years old. The person must be a natural-born US citizen. He or she must also have lived in the United States for at least 14 years.

## Electoral College

The US presidential election is an indirect election. Voters from each state choose electors. These electors represent their state in the Electoral College. Each elector has one electoral vote. Electors cast their vote for the candidate with the highest number of votes from people in their state. A candidate must receive the majority of Electoral College votes to win.

## Term of Office

Each president may be elected to two four-year terms. The presidential election is held on the Tuesday after the first Monday in November. The president is sworn in on January 20 of the following year. At that time, he or she takes the oath of office.
It states:

I do solemnly swear (or affirm) that I will faithfully execute the office of President of the United States, and will to the best of my ability, preserve, protect and defend the Constitution of the United States.

31

# Line of Succession

The Presidential Succession Act of 1947 states who becomes president if the president cannot serve. The vice president is first in the line. Next are the Speaker of the House and the President Pro Tempore of the Senate. It may happen that none of these individuals is able to serve. Then the office falls to the president's cabinet members. They would take office in the order in which each department was created:

Secretary of State

Secretary of the Treasury

Secretary of Defense

Attorney General

Secretary of the Interior

Secretary of Agriculture

Secretary of Commerce

Secretary of Labor

Secretary of Health and Human Services

Secretary of Housing
and Urban Development

Secretary of Transportation

Secretary of Energy

Secretary of Education

Secretary of Veterans Affairs

Secretary of Homeland Security

# Benefits

★ While in office, the president receives a salary. It is $400,000 per year. He or she lives in the White House. The president also has 24-hour Secret Service protection.

★ The president may travel on a Boeing 747 jet. This special jet is called Air Force One. It can hold 70 passengers. It has kitchens, a dining room, sleeping areas, and more. Air Force One can fly halfway around the world before needing to refuel. It can even refuel in flight!

★ When the president travels by car, he or she uses Cadillac One. It is a Cadillac Deville that has been modified. The car has heavy armor and communications systems. The president may even take Cadillac One along when visiting other countries.

★ The president also travels on a helicopter. It is called Marine One. It may also be taken along when the president visits other countries.

★ Sometimes the president needs to get away with family and friends. Camp David is the official presidential retreat. It is located in Maryland. The US Navy maintains the retreat. The US Marine Corps keeps it secure. The camp offers swimming, tennis, golf, and hiking.

★ When the president leaves office, he or she receives lifetime Secret Service protection. He or she also receives a yearly pension of $203,700. The former president also receives money for office space, supplies, and staff.

# PRESIDENTS AND THEIR TERMS

| PRESIDENT | PARTY | TOOK OFFICE | LEFT OFFICE | TERMS SERVED | VICE PRESIDENT |
|---|---|---|---|---|---|
| George Washington | None | April 30, 1789 | March 4, 1797 | Two | John Adams |
| John Adams | Federalist | March 4, 1797 | March 4, 1801 | One | Thomas Jefferson |
| Thomas Jefferson | Democratic-Republican | March 4, 1801 | March 4, 1809 | Two | Aaron Burr, George Clinton |
| James Madison | Democratic-Republican | March 4, 1809 | March 4, 1817 | Two | George Clinton, Elbridge Gerry |
| James Monroe | Democratic-Republican | March 4, 1817 | March 4, 1825 | Two | Daniel D. Tompkins |
| John Quincy Adams | Democratic-Republican | March 4, 1825 | March 4, 1829 | One | John C. Calhoun |
| Andrew Jackson | Democrat | March 4, 1829 | March 4, 1837 | Two | John C. Calhoun, Martin Van Buren |
| Martin Van Buren | Democrat | March 4, 1837 | March 4, 1841 | One | Richard M. Johnson |
| William H. Harrison | Whig | March 4, 1841 | April 4, 1841 | Died During First Term | John Tyler |
| John Tyler | Whig | April 6, 1841 | March 4, 1845 | Completed Harrison's Term | Office Vacant |
| James K. Polk | Democrat | March 4, 1845 | March 4, 1849 | One | George M. Dallas |
| Zachary Taylor | Whig | March 5, 1849 | July 9, 1850 | Died During First Term | Millard Fillmore |

| PRESIDENT | PARTY | TOOK OFFICE | LEFT OFFICE | TERMS SERVED | VICE PRESIDENT |
|---|---|---|---|---|---|
| Millard Fillmore | Whig | July 10, 1850 | March 4, 1853 | Completed Taylor's Term | Office Vacant |
| Franklin Pierce | Democrat | March 4, 1853 | March 4, 1857 | One | William R.D. King |
| James Buchanan | Democrat | March 4, 1857 | March 4, 1861 | One | John C. Breckinridge |
| Abraham Lincoln | Republican | March 4, 1861 | April 15, 1865 | Served One Term, Died During Second Term | Hannibal Hamlin, Andrew Johnson |
| Andrew Johnson | Democrat | April 15, 1865 | March 4, 1869 | Completed Lincoln's Second Term | Office Vacant |
| Ulysses S. Grant | Republican | March 4, 1869 | March 4, 1877 | Two | Schuyler Colfax, Henry Wilson |
| Rutherford B. Hayes | Republican | March 3, 1877 | March 4, 1881 | One | William A. Wheeler |
| James A. Garfield | Republican | March 4, 1881 | September 19, 1881 | Died During First Term | Chester Arthur |
| Chester Arthur | Republican | September 20, 1881 | March 4, 1885 | Completed Garfield's Term | Office Vacant |
| Grover Cleveland | Democrat | March 4, 1885 | March 4, 1889 | One | Thomas A. Hendricks |
| Benjamin Harrison | Republican | March 4, 1889 | March 4, 1893 | One | Levi P. Morton |
| Grover Cleveland | Democrat | March 4, 1893 | March 4, 1897 | One | Adlai E. Stevenson |
| William McKinley | Republican | March 4, 1897 | September 14, 1901 | Served One Term, Died During Second Term | Garret A. Hobart, Theodore Roosevelt |

| PRESIDENT | PARTY | TOOK OFFICE | LEFT OFFICE | TERMS SERVED | VICE PRESIDENT |
|---|---|---|---|---|---|
| **Theodore Roosevelt** | Republican | September 14, 1901 | March 4, 1909 | Completed McKinley's Second Term, Served One Term | Office Vacant, Charles Fairbanks |
| **William Taft** | Republican | March 4, 1909 | March 4, 1913 | One | James S. Sherman |
| **Woodrow Wilson** | Democrat | March 4, 1913 | March 4, 1921 | Two | Thomas R. Marshall |
| **Warren G. Harding** | Republican | March 4, 1921 | August 2, 1923 | Died During First Term | Calvin Coolidge |
| **Calvin Coolidge** | Republican | August 3, 1923 | March 4, 1929 | Completed Harding's Term, Served One Term | Office Vacant, Charles Dawes |
| **Herbert Hoover** | Republican | March 4, 1929 | March 4, 1933 | One | Charles Curtis |
| **Franklin D. Roosevelt** | Democrat | March 4, 1933 | April 12, 1945 | Served Three Terms, Died During Fourth Term | John Nance Garner, Henry A. Wallace, Harry S. Truman |
| **Harry S. Truman** | Democrat | April 12, 1945 | January 20, 1953 | Completed Roosevelt's Fourth Term, Served One Term | Office Vacant, Alben Barkley |
| **Dwight D. Eisenhower** | Republican | January 20, 1953 | January 20, 1961 | Two | Richard Nixon |
| **John F. Kennedy** | Democrat | January 20, 1961 | November 22, 1963 | Died During First Term | Lyndon B. Johnson |
| **Lyndon B. Johnson** | Democrat | November 22, 1963 | January 20, 1969 | Completed Kennedy's Term, Served One Term | Office Vacant, Hubert H. Humphrey |
| **Richard Nixon** | Republican | January 20, 1969 | August 9, 1974 | Completed First Term, Resigned During Second Term | Spiro T. Agnew, Gerald Ford |

| PRESIDENT | PARTY | TOOK OFFICE | LEFT OFFICE | TERMS SERVED | VICE PRESIDENT |
|---|---|---|---|---|---|
| Gerald Ford | Republican | August 9, 1974 | January 20, 1977 | Completed Nixon's Second Term | Nelson A. Rockefeller |
| Jimmy Carter | Democrat | January 20, 1977 | January 20, 1981 | One | Walter Mondale |
| Ronald Reagan | Republican | January 20, 1981 | January 20, 1989 | Two | George H.W. Bush |
| George H.W. Bush | Republican | January 20, 1989 | January 20, 1993 | One | Dan Quayle |
| Bill Clinton | Democrat | January 20, 1993 | January 20, 2001 | Two | Al Gore |
| George W. Bush | Republican | January 20, 2001 | January 20, 2009 | Two | Dick Cheney |
| Barack Obama | Democrat | January 20, 2009 | January 20, 2017 | Two | Joe Biden |

"The great objects of our pursuit as a people are best to be attained by peace."

Franklin Pierce

## ★ WRITE TO THE PRESIDENT ★

**You may write to the president at:**
The White House
1600 Pennsylvania Avenue NW
Washington, DC 20500

**You may e-mail the president at:**
comments@whitehouse.gov

37

# Glossary

**abolition**—the act of ending slavery.

**challenge** (CHA-luhnj)—something that tests one's strengths or abilities.

**Constitution**—the laws that govern the United States.

**Democrat**—a member of the Democratic political party.

**district attorney**—a person who gives the government advice on laws and works in a specific district, such as a county or a state.

**divide**—to separate into two parts.

**expand**—to make larger.

**foreign**—located outside one's own country.

**graduate** (GRA-juh-wayt)—to complete a level of schooling.

**lawyer** (LAW-yuhr)—a person who gives people advice on laws or represents them in court.

**legal**—based on or allowed by law.

**legislature**—group of people with the power to make or change laws.

**Mexican-American War**—a war between the United States and Mexico that lasted from 1846 to 1848.

**politics**—the art or science of government. Something referring to politics is political. A person who is active in politics is a politician.

**recruit**—to get a person to join something.

**representative**—someone chosen in an election to act or speak for the people who voted for him or her.

**reward**—to give something as thanks for or recognition of someone's efforts.

**speaker**—the head officer of a lawmaking assembly.

**support**—to believe in or be in favor of something.

**treaty**—an agreement made between two or more groups.

**Whig Party**—a US political party active between 1834 and 1854.

# ★ WEBSITES ★

To learn more about the US Presidents, visit **booklinks.abdopublishing.com**. These links are routinely monitored and updated to provide the most current information available.

# Index